Cutting-Edge STEM

Cutting-Edge Augmented Reality

Christy Peterson

Lerner Publications ◆ Minneapolis

For E² and J, who make my reality better every day

Lerner Publications Company
A division of Lerner Publishing Group, Inc.
241 First Avenue North
Minneapolis, MN 55401 USA

For reading levels and more information, look up this title
at www.lernerbooks.com.

Main body text set in Adrianna Regular 14/20.
Typeface provided by Chank.

Library of Congress Cataloging-in-Publication Data

Names: Peterson, Christy, author.
Title: Cutting-edge augmented reality / Christy Peterson.
Description: Minneapolis, MN : Lerner Publications, [2019] | Series: Searchlight books.
   Cutting-edge STEM | Includes bibliographical references and index. | Audience: Ages
   8–11. | Audience: Grades 4 to 6.
Identifiers: LCCN 2017061821 (print) | LCCN 2017060527 (ebook) | ISBN 9781541525375
   (eb pdf) | ISBN 9781541523432 (lb : alk. paper) | ISBN 9781541527744 (pb : alk. paper)
Subjects: LCSH: Augmented reality—Juvenile literature.
Classification: LCC QA76.9.A94 (print) | LCC QA76.9.A94 P48 2019 (ebook) | DDC
   006.8—dc23

LC record available at https://lccn.loc.gov/2017061821

Manufactured in the United States of America
1-44416-34675-4/2/2018

Contents

Chapter 1

WHAT IS AUGMENTED REALITY?

Some friends stand together in a park. Their fingers swipe quickly across smartphone screens. One snaps a photo. They laugh and point at their phones. The group is playing *Pokémon Go*. In the game, players toss pretend balls at cartoon Pokémon characters to catch them.

Smartphones have become an important part of everyday life. There are lots of amazing ways to use this technology!

This person plays *Pokémon Go* in a grocery store. The phone's camera shows the real store aisle. The game added the character and ball.

Pokémon Go uses a phone's camera to show a person's real-life surroundings, such as parks, roads, and buildings. The game adds cartoon animals and balls to the real-life scene on the phone's screen. This is an example of augmented reality (AR). Reality is everything in the real world. *Augment* means "to add something."

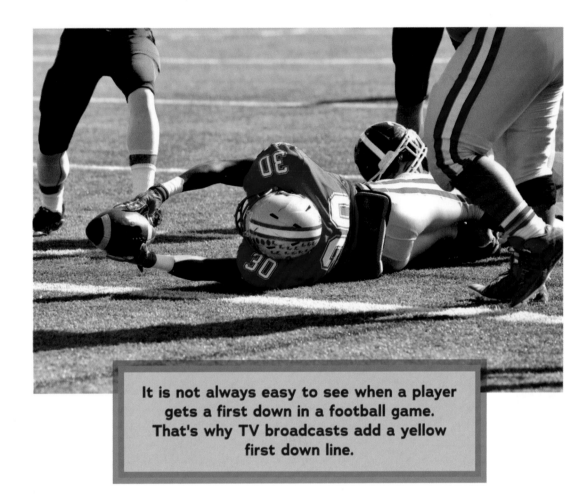

It is not always easy to see when a player gets a first down in a football game. That's why TV broadcasts add a yellow first down line.

Hidden in Plain Sight

Before *Pokémon Go*, many people had never heard of AR. But it has been part of TV sports for a long time. In football games on TV, a yellow first down line appears on the field. There isn't really a line on the field. A computer program adds the line to make it easier for fans to follow the game.

In televised NASCAR races, boxes pop up over the cars. The boxes contain facts about the cars and drivers. A computer program keeps the boxes over the right cars, even though the cars are moving quickly around the track. With AR, the information added by the computer changes as things in the real world change.

NASCAR races include many cars. It can be tricky to keep track of who is winning. But AR helps!

AR Everywhere

These days, we see and use AR in many parts of our lives. Think of something simple, like taking a selfie. You can send a plain photo of yourself to your friends, or you can use an AR program to add bunny ears or a funny nose. The program uses your phone's camera to see where your nose and head are. That's how it puts the nose and ears in the right places in the image.

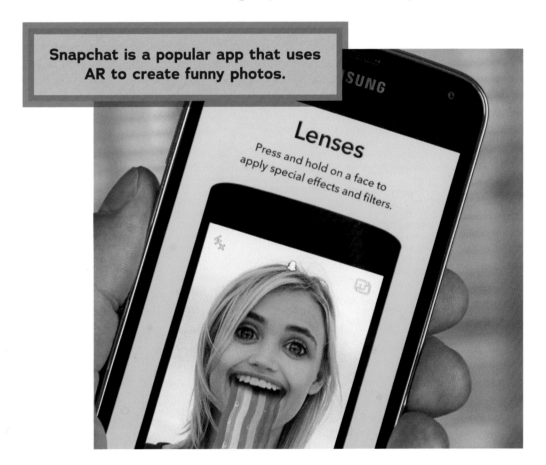

Snapchat is a popular app that uses AR to create funny photos.

Coding Spotlight

A computer program is a set of instructions written in code. The code tells a computer how to do a task. The code for an AR program tells the computer what kind of image to create and how to process information from the real world to place the imagery. People who develop AR programs need excellent computer and design skills to create digital images that move and change with the real world.

Another AR tool helps you shop for new glasses. The program uses a camera to look at your face. It sees your eyes, ears, and nose. It knows to put the glasses over your eyes and not on top of your head! You can try different colors and styles to find the perfect glasses without ever trying on a real pair.

This woman uses an AR program to "try on" a new outfit in a store in Tokyo, Japan.

Chapter 2

AUGMENTED LEARNING

Have you ever loved a book so much that you wished you could jump inside? AR makes this almost possible. An AR book looks perfectly normal. It has words, pictures, and pages. But some pages also have symbols called targets. A computer program can read these targets.

Reading helps you learn and experience new things. AR can make the experience even more vivid.

The program uses the camera on a phone or tablet to see the target. The target tells the program which page you are reading. Then the program creates a picture of a character or object from that page that appears on your screen. Some programs make the object seem to jump out of the page. Others let you zoom in for a closer look. Sometimes the characters even make sounds or move around.

ONE AR PROGRAM CAN MAKE
YOUR OWN DRAWINGS COME TO LIFE!

▼

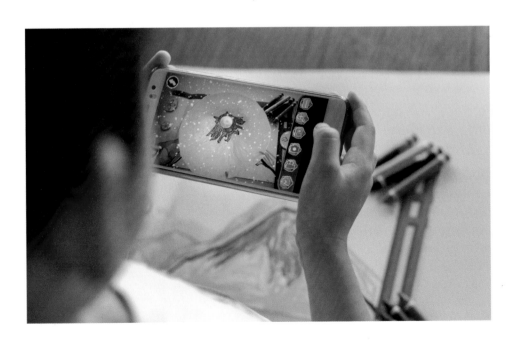

Tour guides tell stories and share extra information to help people learn about an exhibit.

Bringing History to Life

A history museum in Austria has AR targets near some of its exhibits. Visitors look at the targets through tablets or smartphones. A tour guide appears on the screen and tells stories about the bones, weapons, tools, and clothes in the displays. Instead of simply reading signs about the exhibits, visitors can hear and see what life was really like in the past.

It can be difficult to imagine what prehistoric animals really looked like. An AR program can give you a pretty good idea.

A museum in Washington, DC, uses AR to bring animal bones to life. You can point your phone camera at a skeleton. A computer program adds skin and hair to show how the animal looked when it was alive. The program also shows how the bones helped the animal move and eat.

Creating Together

Computer programmers make AR programs to tell a computer how to add words, pictures, and sounds to real life. But programmers don't create these tools alone. Artists, historians, scientists, and writers help too.

Artists, scientists, and programmers at the company Visible Body create AR technology to help students learn about the human body.

The Alamo

Almost two hundred years ago, a fierce battle took place at the Alamo, a fort in San Antonio, Texas. Visitors to the fort can use an AR tool to see what happened there. To create the tool, historians gathered letters, drawings, and old objects. Artists created images of people, buildings, and furniture. Writers wrote stories. And programmers told a computer how to put it together.

A smartphone tells the program where the visitors are. When they get to the exact spot where something happened, the program starts up. It loads stories about people who were there during the battle. People can peek inside rooms and see what they looked like. They can even hear sounds of battle. It's not quite time travel, but it brings the past to life in a brand-new way.

http://bit.ly/imaginevirtua

Try out Imagine Virtua's AR technology! Scan this code with a QR code reader to download an app that brings a battle scene to life.

Science Fact or Science Fiction?

AR lets you send secret messages to your friends.

This is true!

An app called WallaMe lets you leave hidden messages in locations all around the world. Only people using the app can read the message. For example, you can use the app to take a picture of a street and write a message on the image. Other people who look at the same street with their phone's camera can see the message you wrote.

Chapter 3

ON THE JOB

Imagine your job is to help build airplanes. You connect wires that bring electricity to all parts of the plane. In the past, workers had paper drawings to help them place each wire in the right spot. These workers could easily lose their place or make mistakes when they went back and forth between the paper and the wires. But you have a special pair of glasses to help you do the job faster.

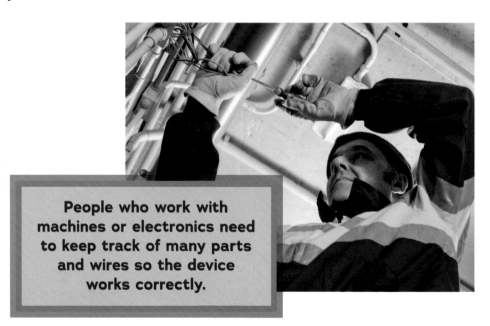

People who work with machines or electronics need to keep track of many parts and wires so the device works correctly.

The glasses are connected to a computer program. A drawing that shows where each wire goes appears on the lenses right in front of your eyes. You can see the real wires in your hand at the same time. If you're stuck, you use the glasses to watch an instruction video.

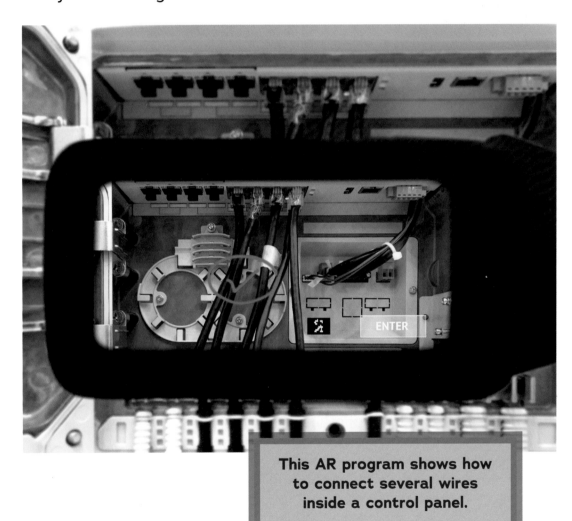

ENTER

This AR program shows how to connect several wires inside a control panel.

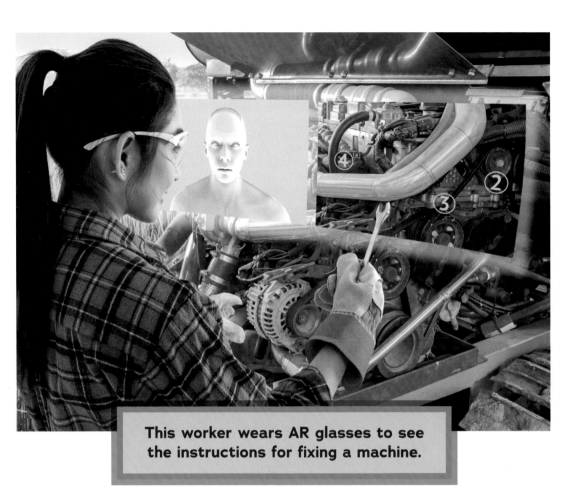

This worker wears AR glasses to see the instructions for fixing a machine.

Repair workers use AR glasses too. They can see a picture of the inside of a machine and instructions for how to fix the broken part. The worker sees the real machine at the same time. If there is a problem, the worker can call for help. The helper can see exactly what the worker is seeing through the glasses to figure out how to fix the problem.

AR at the Doctor

Your doctor probably won't use AR glasses at your next checkup. But some doctors use them. Surgeons often take pictures of people's insides to prepare for surgery. These pictures help the surgeon know what is wrong and how to fix the problem. Using the glasses, surgeons can see these pictures when they look at the patient's body. This helps the surgeon plan the safest way to do the surgery.

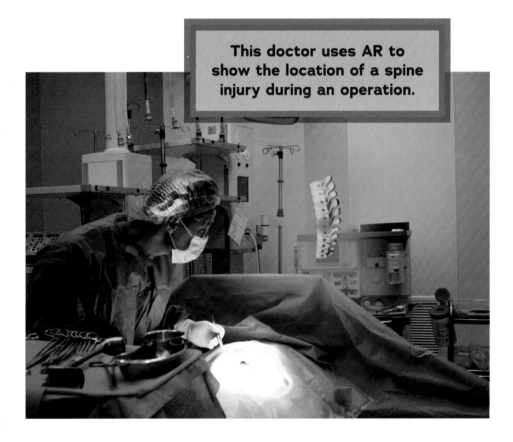

This doctor uses AR to show the location of a spine injury during an operation.

Augmented Reality in Action

Have you ever had your blood drawn? It can be a little scary to see the needle coming your way. It's scarier for people whose veins are hard for a nurse to find. Sometimes a nurse has to try several times before finding a vein. That's no fun at all. An AR tool is helping. The tool allows a nurse to see exactly where the veins are. The nurse can safely draw blood with only one poke.

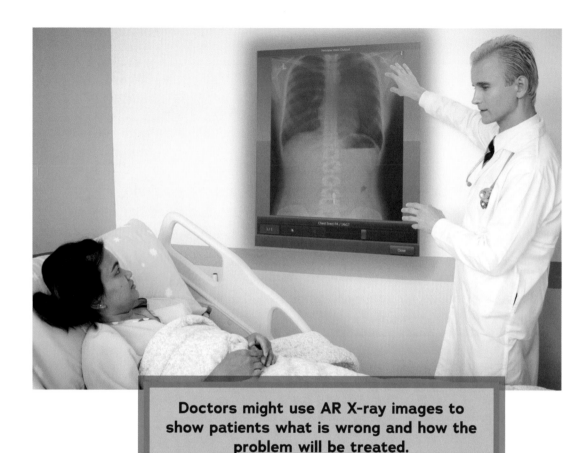

Doctors might use AR X-ray images to show patients what is wrong and how the problem will be treated.

Sometimes people need surgery to save their lives. But what if the best doctor for that kind of surgery lives far away? AR glasses can help. The glasses allow doctors in different parts of the world to work together. Other doctors can see what the surgeon sees. They can talk about what to do next. Together they can save the patient.

Chapter 4

EVERYDAY REALITY

A few years ago, people waiting for a bus in London, England, got a big surprise. Through the window of the bus shelter, some saw alien ships. Others watched a sea creature come out of a hole in the sidewalk. Not everything they saw was real, of course. The window of the bus shelter was really a giant screen. The pictures of the sidewalk were real. An AR program added everything else.

AR could make a long wait at the bus stop much more exciting!

What's Next?

Experts predict AR will soon be as common as smartphones and computers. Car companies are trying out windshields that are also AR screens. Drivers won't have to look away from the road to see how fast they are going or where to turn next. AR map programs won't just show buildings and street names. They'll also display information about the businesses inside each building. AR programs will be tools people use every day to interact with the world.

This image shows what AR might look like on a car's windshield. Companies around the world have been developing this technology that shows speed and gives directions to a driver.

82 kph

30 M

40 M

450 M

Science Fact or Science Fiction?

AR lets you understand any language.

Well, this isn't quite true—yet.

In science fiction stories, universal translators let humans and aliens speak to each other. But people are working to make real translators. That won't help with aliens, but it could help if you are traveling in another country! One tool lets you read signs written in other languages. You can look at a sign using your phone, and the program will show you the words in the language you understand.

A boy tries out Google Glass, a device that shows information right in front of your eyes.

Some people think AR technology might be placed inside our bodies. They think screens might be put into our eyes. Or wires will be inserted directly into our brains. With a blink of our eyes or a simple thought, we would be able to find the information we need.

There are ways to use AR that no one has thought of yet. So start dreaming big. How do you think AR could make the world a better place? Who knows? The person who dreams up the next amazing AR tool could be you!

Students at a university in Thailand are learning to develop AR technology.

Glossary

augmented reality (AR): a combination of real life and information added by a computer

computer program: a set of instructions that tells a computer how to do a task

museum: a building where important objects of art, history, or science are stored and displayed

programmer: a person who writes instructions that tell a computer what to do

selfie: a picture you take of yourself, usually with a smartphone or tablet

surgery: a medical process for repairing, removing, or replacing parts of a person's body

translator: a person or device that changes a word from one language to another

Learn More about Augmented Reality

Books

Martin, Brett S. *Augmented Reality*. Chicago: Norwood House, 2017. Find out more about the technology behind augmented reality.

Peterson, Christy. *Cutting-Edge Virtual Reality*. Minneapolis: Lerner Publications, 2019. Learn about another amazing technology that is changing the way we view the world.

Silverman, Buffy. *The World of Pokémon*. Minneapolis: Lerner Publications, 2018. Read this book to find out more about the game that made augmented reality so well known.

Websites

Kinooze: What Is Augmented Reality?
http://kinooze.com/what-is-augmented-reality/
Watch videos and read more about how augmented reality works and how people can use it.

Scratch
https://scratch.mit.edu/tips
Create your own digital elements with this learn-to-code website. You can even place digital elements on a real-world background.

Smithsonian: Skin and Bones
http://naturalhistory.si.edu/exhibits/bone-hall/
See how augmented reality works at the Smithsonian's Museum of Natural History, and try it out yourself!

Index

Photo Acknowledgments

The images in this book are used with the permission of: Syda Productions/Shutterstock.com, p. 4; Wachiwit/Shutterstock.com, p. 5; JoeSAPhotos/Shutterstock.com, p. 6; Daniel Hurlimann/Shutterstock.com, p. 7; dennizn/Shutterstock.com, p. 8; JEAN-FRANCOIS MONIER/AFP/Getty Images, p. 9; YOSHIKAZU TSUNO/AFP/Getty Images, p. 10; IAM PRAWIT/Shutterstock.com, p. 11; Freer/Shutterstock.com, p. 12; Monkey Business Images/Shutterstock.com, p. 13; cowardlion/Shutterstock.com, p. 14; David L. Ryan/The Boston Globe/Getty Images, p. 15; f11photo/Shutterstock.com, p. 16; © 2018 Alamo Reality. Created by Imagine Virtua for Alamo Reality, p. 17 (foreground); SchnepfDesign/Shutterstock.com, p. 17 (background); Thavorn Rueang/Shutterstock.com, p. 18; alfernec/Shutterstock.com, p. 19; Zapp2Photo/Shutterstock.com, pp. 20, 21; Beros919/Shutterstock.com, pp. 22, 24; Leonie Broekstra/Shutterstock.com, p. 23; photodonato/Shutterstock.com, p. 25; Ekkasit Keatsirikul/Alamy Stock Photo, p. 26; supparsorn/Shutterstock.com, p. 27; Timothy Fadek/Corbis/Getty Images, p. 28; Narin Nonthamand/Shutterstock.com, p. 29.

Front cover: Freer/Shutterstock.com.